This journal belongs to:

....

Contents

A note from the editor

Finding joy in all things, big and small, is easy once you know how. Let us guide you on your gratitude journey for a happier, more fulfilled life

We've all been guilty of comparing ourselves to others at some point in our lives. It's human nature. We've most likely all uttered (or at least mentally uttered) the words "It's so unfair"; "They're so lucky"; or "I wish I had/could do…" This doesn't make us terrible people; if anything, it demonstrates ambition and aspiration, maybe even leading to the motivation to make positive changes happen. However, having these thoughts too often can make us lose sight of the here and now, and what we *do* have. Constantly striving for more is fine if you appreciate what you've already got, but many of us simply don't. And getting caught in this trap doesn't necessarily make us "ungrateful," it just means our lives could be improved and enriched by being *more* grateful more often.

Practicing gratitude goes beyond simply thanking someone for something they've done. It's an art that involves taking a step back, pausing, and mindfully taking stock of what's in your life and what's important in your life. This acknowledgment then leads to a whole host of questions to consider. Why do I value this so much? What does this person bring to my life? How would my life be worse without…? There are significant things to be grateful for, such as having a job, recovering well from an operation, or your children getting into their first-choice school, for example. But then there are the more subtle things that pepper goodness into our everyday lives, such as having fresh running water to make a hot drink, living close to a family member or friend, having a garden to hang the laundry in, and so on. By appreciating the big and the small, we soon become happy with the abundance of positive things in our lives.

If practicing gratitude is a new concept to you, there is plenty of advice in this book to help you get started, and getting started will be the hardest part. Once you understand what's required and are equipped with all the necessary tools, practicing gratitude will become second nature, and that's when you'll really notice the benefits in your everyday life.

The first section of this book highlights examples of things you might want to consider before you embark on the journal itself, such as people, health, hobbies and much more. Then when you feel ready to start recording your thoughts, turn to the journal pages and start writing. You'll find tips and activities that break up the journal pages and provide inspirational ideas to ensure you don't slip back into old habits. Enjoy!

Sarah Bankes

Editor

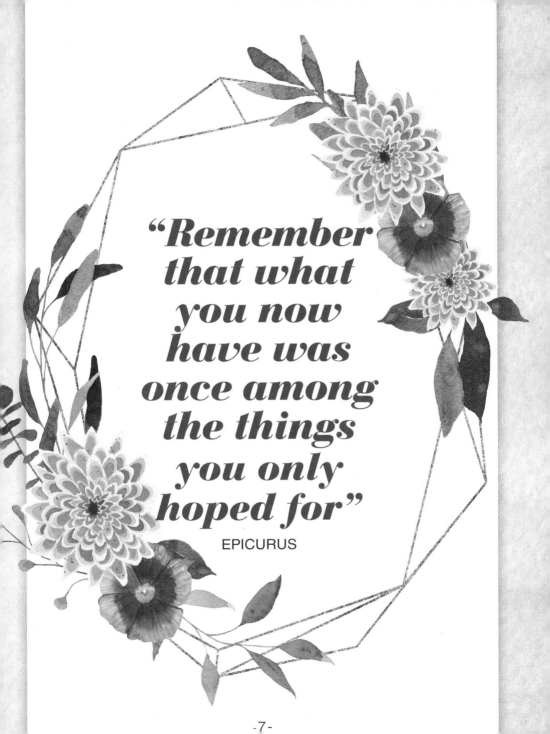

"Remember that what you now have was once among the things you only hoped for"

EPICURUS

The power of gratitude

Gratitude is a magical tool that we should all be tapping into more frequently. You'll soon begin to see there are so many reasons to be grateful – you just have to allow yourself the time to notice them

How many times have you found something irritating today? How many times have you focused on the negative things that have happened? Now how many times have you made a mental note of something positive that happened? We are all guilty of focusing on life's tiny burdens instead of remaining mindful of our blessings and how lucky we are to be alive. For many years, gratitude has played an important part in a lot of religious and spiritual practices as a way of connecting us to the present moment and reaffirming how precious life can be. Whether you believe in destiny or not, sometimes it might feel as though we have little control over which direction our lives are going. But gratitude teaches us that we have a choice about what we focus our attention on. By making time to write gratitude lists, we gain control over our minds, forcing ourselves to focus on the good rather than the bad.

According to author Eckhart Tolle, "the mind exists in a state of 'not enough' and so [it] is always greedy for more." Our minds are continuously in overdrive, striving for the next best thing – whether that's a new car, a new pair of shoes or the latest tech device. We are always trying to better ourselves in one way or another. In doing so, we might have become a bit lost and forgotten what truly makes us content. But hope is not lost just yet. What we can all be doing more of is stopping to appreciate what we already have around us. In the modern, technology-filled world, our minds are being stimulated more than ever, and sometimes this can mean that we find ourselves turning to consumerism

> *"Let us rise up and be thankful, for if we didn't learn a lot today, at least we learned a little, and if we didn't learn a little, at least we didn't get sick, and if we got sick, at least we didn't die; so, let usall be thankful"*
>
> **LEO BUSCAGLIA**

for an instant "fix" to enrich our lives. In doing so, we bypass the most simple fact – that life is full to the brim of moments of joy that money cannot buy. Gratitude teaches us to stop, pause and reflect on our own lives and be thankful for all that we have. Gratitude also steers our attention away from negativity and instead focuses on the hidden treasures that can be found in the simple pleasures of life.

Why is gratitude important in the modern world?

Over the course of the last 100 years, we have forgotten how to find pleasure in the everyday things in life. Through no fault of our own, modern life has become increasingly more complicated, stressful and busy, which is why it's more important than ever for us to strip everything back and remind ourselves of what truly gives us purpose, makes us tick and brings a smile to our faces. Life can become crazy from time to time, with many of us struggling to manage our own schedules efficiently and find balance between our professional and personal lives. It is here in the humdrum that some of us may have lost sight of what is actually important to us. Take a moment now and think about your typical day.

Great gratitude apps

Left the house without your gratitude journal? Going away for the weekend but want to remember all the highlights? There are some great apps out there that enable you to quickly document your gratitude. Here are our top three that you can use while out and about – but don't forget to update your journal when you return.

Five Minute Journal
Available on iOS & Android
Price: $4.99

Morning!
Available on iOS
Price: Free

Grateful
Available on iOS
Price: Free (in-app purchases)

Do you frequently reach the evening wondering "where did the day go?" Are you pausing to appreciate the great moments that you have experienced over the course of the day? Did you make a note of them? If you answered no to the latter questions, then the good news is you've come to the right place. It's time to start appreciating everything life has to offer, and this journal is here to help.

The power of pausing, slowing down and living in the present moment

When life becomes busy and hectic, it can be very easy to live our lives on autopilot, but in doing so we miss all the best bits. This is where gratitude becomes invaluable, as it helps to redirect us when we feel a bit lost. Whenever we're overwhelmed or feeling down, gratitude forces us to concentrate on the here and now and remind ourselves of life's simple pleasures. This gratitude journal will provide you with a safe space to reflect from time to time, enabling you to focus on the present moment and appreciate the small things that spark contentment in your life. Allowing yourself this time for contemplation every now and again lets you shine a light on all of the positive elements in your life – even when it might feel like there aren't any. You'll soon find that there is a lot more to be grateful for than you first thought.

Gratitude comes in all shapes and sizes

We all have different things that we are grateful for day to day. Many people would consider similar themes: family, friends, health, love and having a place to

"*Your joy,
your
misery,
your love,
your agony,
your bliss,
lie in your
hands*"

SADHGURU

call home. These are all valid, of course, but why specifically are we grateful for them? Perhaps one of the main reasons you've picked up this journal is that you are struggling to find everyday things to be grateful for. Maybe you're finding it hard to pinpoint exactly what made you happy today. These are all common feelings, and are no doubt some of the hurdles that you might encounter as you work through this journal.

The good news is that you are not alone – we all have good days and bad days. Sometimes our happiest moments on the tough days are as simple as crawling into bed after a long day at work, or enjoying a cup of coffee in the morning. Life is complicated enough – you don't need to make things harder for yourself by trying to think of interesting anecdotes or original content for each entry. Let's strip everything back and get down to the basic elements of your life because, more often than not, the simple things in life are the things that make us the happiest.

Share the love

As we go through life, we might forget how important some of the key people in our lives truly are. You might find when writing in this journal that you are frequently grateful for people. Most of us have a small support network of friends and family members who continuously show up for us. It's more important than ever that we let these people know how invaluable they are to our mental health and overall happiness, so don't hesitate to tell them and show them some love.

The newfound joy of simple things

One of the many benefits of gratitude is its ability to teach us how to slow down in our fast-paced lives. A big problem with our constant consumption of entertainment and our over-stimulation in the digital world is that we are forgetting how to stop and notice the small things. We are unintentionally living on fast forward and not acknowledging how beautiful our lives are.

Over the course of writing in this journal, you might find that you begin to feel grateful for something that you

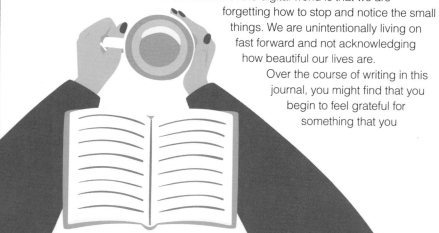

wouldn't have necessarily noticed before. Some of these small pleasures could be stopping and appreciating the wonderful flavors in your dinner, that cuddle with a loved one, the fresh air in your local park, or the first signs of autumn. But just because you are stopping to take note of all the little mundane things in life, it doesn't mean you have to ignore all of the life-changing moments. Some examples of big moments that can often make us feel overwhelmed with gratitude are birthdays, weddings and personal achievements. Whether big or small, it's important we pause and appreciate everything that life has to offer – blink and you might miss it!

Don't discount the tough times

The more we practice gratitude, the better we can prepare ourselves for the tough times that lie ahead, because it is on these days that we arguably need it the most. We will all encounter hardship in our lives at some stage, but it takes sadness to know happiness. These hard moments in life can be anything from mourning the loss of a loved one, to experiencing ill health, to being made redundant. Or they can be something smaller like failing a test or feeling as though you've let a friend down. But just because you've encountered bumps in the road, it doesn't mean that you should discount them as bad days, because it is here that we build resilience and strength, and gain perspective on the things that truly matter in life. You can also be grateful for the hardships, because it is here that we are forced to really dig deep to find the positives and appreciate the beauty that surrounds us.

You can tailor this journal to suit your needs, and you can use gratitude to help shape you into the person you want to become. By shifting your perspective and teaching yourself how to be grateful for everything, including the bad stuff, you will no doubt begin to improve your mental health. Because at the end of the day, there is solace in the fact that the sun continues to rise and set every day, bringing with it a chance to start anew. So instead of focusing on the negative elements, try to

"Stand still. The trees ahead and bush beside you are not lost"

ECKHART TOLLE

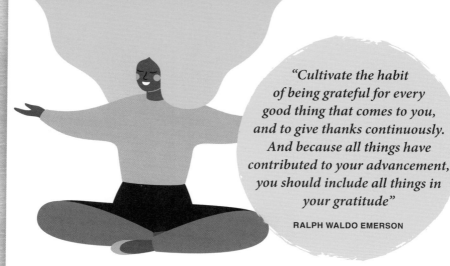

> *"Cultivate the habit of being grateful for every good thing that comes to you, and to give thanks continuously. And because all things have contributed to your advancement, you should include all things in your gratitude"*
>
> **RALPH WALDO EMERSON**

instead see the bad days in a positive light, since they have provided you with space to grow. Use the bad moments to challenge yourself and see them as an opportunity to make peace with your past, learn from mistakes and better yourself.

Positive thinking is all it's cracked up to be

Writing down all of the happy moments, life lessons and fragments of joy helps us to steer ourselves to a happier state of mind. Through gratitude, we teach ourselves to pay more attention to all of the positive aspects of our lives that we otherwise take for granted. By training our minds to focus on the good, we can begin to pave the way for our own journey to happiness. So what are you waiting for? Grab a pen and start becoming more grateful today.

Think about gratitude when buying

You can apply the principles of gratitude when you're first buying an item. If you take the time to think about what you are buying and why, you will make much better purchasing decisions. Are you buying something because you want it or need it, or both? What will this object add to your life and what benefits will it bring? Rather than impulse buying, you're now making informed and well-thought-out decisions that you are in control of. When you use the new item, you can reflect on how it's benefiting you, and be grateful that you took the time to make the right decision when you bought it.

My intentions

Why have you decided to keep a gratitude journal?
Set out your intentions of what you would like to get out of this practice

Begin your journey

Before completing your journal, let's take a look at what's important to you. We all have things or people to be grateful for, but often these thoughts get lost in the busyness of our everyday lives. It's time to pause, notice and appreciate them.

Love yourself

You are a completely unique person made up of individual traits that shape your life and your experiences. Here's how to be grateful for your own wonderful self

When practicing gratitude, we tend to focus on the things and people around us. We might feel grateful for our family and friends, the home we live in or the food on our plates. It's easier in some ways to be grateful for those things that we can touch, feel and experience. We don't often turn inward and reflect on what we're grateful for when it comes to ourselves. We might think about things like good health, but what about who we are innately as a person?

Our personality and our traits are unique to us, so they're worth celebrating. Rather than focusing on the things you don't like about yourself, or the things you can't do, look at what you love about yourself instead. Are you creative? Are you an avid reader? Do you like cooking? Are you kind? Are you a good friend? Figuring out what makes us great can help us to feel better about ourselves. Negative thinking leads to negative feelings, so it stands to reason that looking at yourself positively can lift your mood.

> *"Simply give to yourselves that which you need – which is love and appreciation without judgment"*
>
> **RÉNÉ GAUDETTE**

We all too often rely on others to give us the love and support that we need. The problem with this is that they might not always be around when we need a boost. However, if you learn to love yourself and be grateful for who you are, you can tap into an endless resource of love whenever you need it.

It does take practice though. When you achieve something that you've worked for, don't forget to congratulate yourself and allow yourself to feel proud. It was *you* who did the hard graft, studied, researched or learned, so you should give yourself credit. You might feel like this is being arrogant if you're not used to "talking yourself up," but it's not. It's simply giving yourself the recognition you deserve; a little self-appreciation goes a long way.

Ask others for help

If you find it hard to think positively about yourself and find those things you're grateful for, why not start by asking friends and family? They will tell you what they love about you, which gives you a much better insight into who you are as a person. It can be a very uplifting and positive experience. This gives you a starting point of the types of areas you can focus your gratitude on. Keep a list somewhere safe of these good points so you can refer back to them on days when you feel low.

Gratitude for your body

It can be really hard to feel grateful for our bodies when we're surrounded by diet culture on social media and in magazines. But your body is so important and enables you to do so much. It's time to switch up the narrative and start to love your physical self for what it can do beyond the aesthetics – it's the only body you'll ever have, after all! Take a look in the mirror and find your personal positives. What do you like about yourself and what do you feel thankful for? You might want to write these things down and stick them on that same mirror as a reminder on days you feel down about your body.

Take time to reflect

We often forget to look back on the amazing things we've achieved. It's really important to take stock of how we have grown and developed. Have you learned a new skill in the last year? What has that enabled you to do that gives you joy or that you're proud of? Have you started a new exercise class and stuck with it? How does that make you feel? Have you made new friends, increased your energy or lifted your mood by attending? Set aside a day to focus on yourself, and write down what has happened in the last year that you are thankful for.

I am proud of...

What have you achieved in your life that you are most proud of?

Love yourself

List what you love most about yourself,
such as physical attributes or parts of your personality

....

....

....

....

....

....

....

....

....

Your loved ones

Here's why and how we could all do with slowing down a bit more, and pausing to take note of some of the incredible people in our lives

The average person will meet upward of 10,000 people in a lifetime, but only a handful of these people will remain close enough to weather life's trials and tribulations with us. Building nourishing relationships is something we learn from as early as childhood through our parental bonds and siblings.

As we mature through adolescence and into adult life, we continue building relationships with various people from all avenues of our lives, and some of these remain crucial companions for us. Maybe you have an idea in your mind now of some of the people you can always rely on in times of need – through the good times and the bad. Whether that is a sibling, parent, friend or partner, that person has no doubt left an irreplaceable mark on you and has helped to shape who you are today. Is that person always there for you when you're having a bad day? Or maybe you're grateful for somebody's energy, because being around them sparks joy and laughter in you? As we go about our everyday lives, it can be very easy to

> *"Let us be grateful to the people who make us happy; they are the charming gardeners who make our souls blossom"*
>
> **MARCEL PROUST**

Why is it beneficial to stop and appreciate the people in our lives?

We've all dealt with the heartbreak of losing a loved one at some stage in our lives, which is why it's crucial we stop to appreciate the people around us today, because tomorrow is never promised. Life can be a chaotic whirlwind of balancing work with everyday life, but pausing to take stock of how lucky we are is key to not only our own happiness but for our loved ones around us too. There is no better feeling than being loved and valued, which is why we should frequently express our gratitude toward the special people in our lives, so they can bask in our appreciation for them.

take these people for granted, but it's important to take note of how vital these people are to our general happiness and overall emotional well-being. Take a moment here to appreciate all the people who add value to your life and continuously show you love and kindness. But our relationships aren't purely with humans – we also form unique bonds with our pets.

Whether it's your dog, cat, rabbit or fish, our pets are examples of unconditional love. It's vital we pause to acknowledge them, too, as we rely on them as much as they do us. Sometimes it can be as simple as recognizing the pure joy that comes from stroking our fluffy friends at the end of a long day at work. Take the time to show your pet how grateful you are for them – whether that's taking your dog for an extra-long walk, or buying your rabbit a tasty treat.

How can you show gratitude to people?

Perhaps while reading this you have identified a person in your life who you are grateful for but you are unsure of how to express your gratitude? The good news is more often than not the most simple gestures are the most effective. Try to avoid any monetary-fueled gifts, but instead shower that person with some well-deserved attention. Sometimes it can be as simple as spending some quality time with them. Or maybe it's just taking your partner a cup of tea in bed or cooking them their favorite meal. If none of these sound up your alley, then why not send a simple text to a close friend or family member telling them how grateful you are for them?

People I love

Make a note below of three people you are most grateful for in your life

1 ....
2 ....
3 ....

Why I love them

Take the first person you've mentioned and note down three traits you love about them

1 ....

....

2 ....

....

3 ....

....

How to show them

Write down three things you can do to show kindness to that person today

1 ....

....

2 ....

....

3 ....

....

Life's important lessons

Why it's crucial we are grateful for all of the experiences
life throws at us – both good and bad

Initially when we think of being grateful, we think of the good things that have been thrown our way. Maybe you are grateful for an experience of learning a new skill; for taking part in charity work; or for being offered the opportunity to embark on a once-in-a-lifetime vacation. Our lives are filled with so many fantastic experiences that make us feel energized, happy and lucky to be alive. But sadly, life is not as linear as we may wish it to be, and along with all of these happy experiences sometimes come the sad and challenging ones too.

A negative experience can be anything that has caused grief, loss, shame, heartbreak or guilt to form. It can be terribly hard to find the light at the end of the tunnel when we are going through painful experiences, but ultimately they are a phenomenal act of strength as you push through and persevere to whatever greater plan is in store for you. A life well lived isn't ever void of negative experiences, and in fact these experiences are just as important as the jovial ones, for they help to teach us vital life lessons. The bad encounters are arguably shaping you into who you are today, so be grateful for them too.

By looking back on some of our most memorable experiences, and being thankful for them, we can take note of how far we have come – not only in our self development but also on our journey to finding happiness and enlightenment. Give yourself some time now to look back over the last year at all the memories and experiences you have collected, and stop to appreciate how lucky you are to have been offered those opportunities.

Don't forget about the smaller experiences too!

Of course, it's easy to focus on the huge, significant experiences we've had in our lives, but it's important to notice the smaller, everyday experiences too. Life can be mundane at times, so pausing to appreciate the little things enables us to tap into the same feelings of bliss. It can be as simple as acknowledging the joy you felt on your commute today. Maybe you cycle to work and you felt the warmth of the sunshine on your back. Or perhaps you experienced the sound of birdsong this morning as you opened a window. Whatever it might be, pause and appreciate its beauty and the joy that it is giving you on yet another potentially ordinary day.

Time to reflect

Identify a painful experience you've had and write down the lesson(s) it taught you below

....

....

....

....

....

....

....

....

....

Learn from the past

Write down three experiences you are most grateful for

1 ....

....

....

2 ....

....

....

3 ....

....

....

Happiness is within

External experiences are building blocks to life, but your internal experience is vital to your everyday existence and your overall happiness. Your internal experience is through the relationship you have with your mind and body. Throughout your day, you're bound to have mindless chatter in your brain, but it's about learning to switch off the negativity and anything that is unproductive to your growth. Instead, make your mind a happy place to be by showing yourself some love and gratitude.

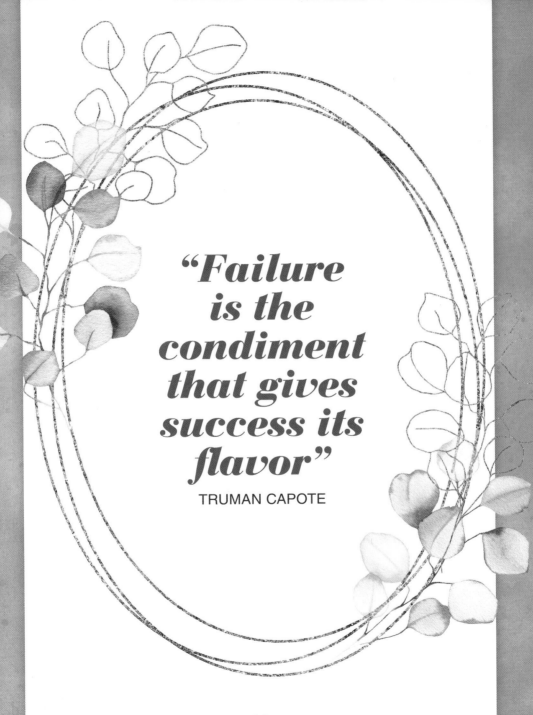

"*Failure
is the
condiment
that gives
success its
flavor*"

TRUMAN CAPOTE

Find your happy place

We can travel to some of the world's best hidden gems,
but sometimes the places we are most grateful for
are the ones found right on our doorsteps

O ver the course of our lives, we will undoubtedly form bonds with many places – from idyllic beaches and bustling cities to unpolished, quirky towns. Some of these places will remain in our memories and in our hearts forever, and like all things special, they will leave unforgettable impressions on us. These places may be at far-flung corners of the world where you shared a magical vacation, built incredible memories and met inspiring people. But more often than not, we form lasting connections with places closer to home because, after all, home is where the heart is.

Sometimes we can be just as grateful, if not more so, for the comfort found in our own homes, where we can relax after a long day at work and feel safe among our loved ones. Some examples of other places that we often feel

Why should we all be grateful for Mother Nature?

Mother Nature has provided us with some incredible places to marvel at. From mountain ranges that span horizons, rolling hillsides that line the countryside, and vast oceans that many species call home. Being among Mother Nature allows us to feel total freedom and contentment as we immerse ourselves in the great outdoors. Every once in a while we should pause and give thanks to Mother Nature for the countless delight she provides us with worldwide. Let's show Mother Nature the love and respect she deserves by leaving behind only footprints so others can enjoy her boundless beauty for years to come.

grateful for are a local beach, a nearby park or even our comfy bed!

Often, one of the best ways to spark a feeling of gratitude is to take yourself to a place that resonates with you and sit and appreciate how lucky it makes you feel. As we meander through life, it's important we stop every once in a while to recognize these special places and express our gratitude for how they have enabled us to feel and the memories we have built there. Do you have a special place in mind? Does that particular place spark happy memories for you? Or does your memorable place just allow you to escape from the stresses of modern life? What makes your place so special is that the memories you have formed there are totally unique to you. So next time you find yourself in a moment of despair, take yourself to your happy place and spend some time there, allowing those powerful feelings of love and gratitude to wash over you.

> *"To feel is to go to the places you were"*
>
> **WILL ADVISE**

Home sweet home

Write three reasons why you are grateful for where you live

1 ....

....

2 ....

....

3 ....

....

My sanctuary

Write about your favorite place to relax and unwind after a hard day

....

....

....

....

How to access your happy place without actually going there

Photographs are wonderful things – they are moments frozen in time and they enable us to travel back to them in our mind. They also enable us to tap into a series of memories and emotions that surround that particular point. In the space below, stick down a photograph of your favorite place or the place you are most grateful for. When you have a bad day, turn to this page and tap into those magical moments you have had there, and allow yourself to feel a plethora of emotions without even having to leave the house.

Paste your photo here

Favorite places

Write about the top three places that make you happy
and why they are important to you

1 ....
....
....
....
....

2 ....
....
....
....
....

3 ....
....
....
....
....

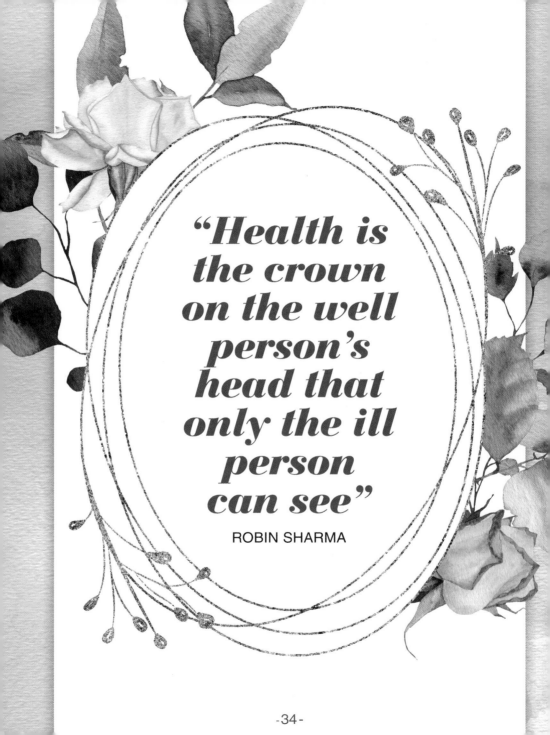

"**Health is the crown on the well person's head that only the ill person can see**"

ROBIN SHARMA

To good health

Being thankful for our physical and mental health isn't just
about being fit and well; it's what our health enables us
to achieve day to day

Many of us pay little attention to our health day to day. We only tend to really think about it when we're in poor health. We notice when we're feeling low or sick, or are injured, because it prevents us from doing our normal, everyday activities. We might also feel grateful for our own good health when someone we know is ill or even sadly passes away – these events make us take stock of our own lives.

However, it's important to focus on our health at all times, and not just when we are suffering or watching the suffering of others. Being grateful for good physical and mental health means so much more than simply being happy to be alive and well. Our health is what enables us to do simple, everyday things. For example, when you go for a walk, moving your body, taking in the sights and sounds of nature, feeling stress slip away… this is all possible because of your good health. Your body is strong enough and capable enough to make the physical steps; your eyes and ears are alert and well so you can experience what is around you; your ability to switch off mentally helps you feel refreshed and calm. Our good health gives us freedom and the capacity to interact with the world around us.

It's more than just physical health. Our brain health, for example, gives us the ability to think and learn, to perform well at work, to play with our children, to engage in conversation. Our logical and cognitive powers help us to read books, learn new skills, engage in hobbies, understand maps so we can travel. It's easy to look at what you can't do. Instead, think about what your body and mind enable you to do. Even a simple task like making a cup of coffee requires coordination and a basic set of processes in the brain. As you enjoy that first sip, be grateful that your body allows you to indulge in these daily pleasures.

The little things

List five simple daily activities you enjoy that
are possible because of your good health

1 ....

2 ....

3 ....

4 ....

5 ....

The gratitude health cycle

Being grateful can lower levels of stress, aid your sleep and help you to feel more connected in your life. So the very act of gratitude can enhance your health and well-being. By being grateful for these aspects of your good health, you can start a beneficial cycle – be thankful for your current good health, which in turn helps you to reap the benefits of gratitude, which in turn gives you even more to be thankful for.

Happy & healthy

I am grateful for my good physical health, because it enables me to…

....

....

....

....

....

....

....

Reflect

Look back on when you were last unwell or injured.
How could you have practiced gratitude for your health at the time?

....

....

....

....

....

....

....

....

....

....

Staying thankful when unwell

It's difficult to show gratitude toward your health when you're feeling poorly. It's not uncommon to feel sorry for ourselves, frustrated that we have to miss out on activities we usually enjoy and watch the world passing us by. However, you can still work on being thankful. When you're unwell, prioritize rest, sleep, good food and water. Be thankful that your body has the means to fight off illness, if you give it the right tools to do so. Enable your body to go through its amazing recovery process, and remember to show thankfulness when you are well again.

Being grateful for "things"

Practicing gratitude doesn't mean living a minimalist existence;
you can still be thankful for physical possessions that help
to make your life easier and more enjoyable

All too often, the art of gratitude is tied in with a minimalist lifestyle. Not relying on material possessions and being thankful for friends, family, good health and the natural world. And while it's accurate to say that being reliant on possessions for our happiness, or getting caught up in materialism and buying things we don't need, isn't ideal for our mental health and well-being, there is a place in our lives to feel grateful for things.

The physical objects around us bring us many benefits that can enhance our lives. It's different for each and every one of us as to what we are thankful for the most. For some, being grateful for a car is a passport to freedom, the ability to visit places as a

"Be thankful for what you have; you'll end up having more. If you concentrate on what you don't have, you will never, ever have enough"

OPRAH WINFREY

Think about gratitude when buying

You can apply the principles of gratitude when you're first buying an item. If you take the time to think about what you are buying and why, you will make much better purchasing decisions. Are you buying something because you want it, or need it, or both? What will this object add to your life and what benefits will it bring? As opposed to impulse buying, you're now making informed and well-thought-out decisions of which you are in control. When you use the new item, you can reflect on how it's benefiting you and be grateful that you took the time to make the right buying decision in the first place.

Focus on what you have

In today's materialistic society, sometimes we can feel the pressure to have the latest car, the newest phone or fashionable clothing. It is this aspect of owning possessions that can lead to negative thoughts and feelings. If we fixate on what we want and not what we have, we're no longer living in the moment. We might feel that we can't keep up with friends or peers. If you switch your mind to what you have and focus your gratitude on that, you will start to feel more positive. A phone enables you to stay in touch with people, whether it's the latest model or a couple of years old, for example.

family or save on commuting time. It's not the car itself that we're thankful for as such, but how that single possession can add so much value to our lives.

When you look around you, you will likely notice things that mean a lot to you for various reasons. Books might bring you endless hours slipping away into a different world, helping to relieve stress and bring joy. A digital device, like a tablet, might help you to connect with other people all around the world. A slow cooker might free up time in the kitchen after work so that you can instead spend that time chatting to your family about your day.

It's not just about convenience and benefits though; some possessions bring us joy for sentimental reasons. A treasured toy from your childhood; a necklace that was a gift; a wedding ring; a photo album filled with memories… these things make us happy and evoke memories and feelings, for which we should be thankful.

The most important thing of all, though, is to let go of guilt for feeling grateful for the things in your life. It's okay to give thanks to material objects. And sometimes, just the act of reflection regarding objects and what they mean to us, can give them far more value than a simple price tag ever could.

My favorite things

Think about three physical possessions you're grateful for and why

1 ....

....

....

2 ....

....

....

3 ....

....

....

Try before you buy

Think of some questions to ask yourself before you buy something new

....

....

....

....

....

....

Treasured items

What material items in your home evoke the most powerful memories?
Make a list of some of these items and how they make you feel

....
....
....
....
....
....
....
....
....
....
....
....
....
....
....

The world around you

Our planet is vast, and sometimes we have to take
a step back to appreciate the good it brings

If you pay too much attention to the news headlines, you start thinking the world is a pretty terrible place to be. However, once you step back and take stock, you soon realize there is so much to be grateful for.

For a start, there is the natural world that we live in. This planet is pretty beautiful if you take the time to notice it. We have unique flora and fauna no matter where we reside. We have access to water and food grown on the land. We have dramatic coastlines and deep forests, sandy beaches and towering mountains. All this in itself can bring a lot to your life and is worth showing gratitude toward.

And then there are the contributions that humanity has made to the wider world. Here in the Western world, we have fresh running water in our homes and when we're out and about. It's easy to dismiss something as simple as water when we have it, and to not really think about it. But if you're ever without access to a clean source of water, you realize its importance. The same goes for things like sanitation, medical facilities, roads that connect places, bridges over water… Human inventions over the years have helped to improve and enhance the lives of us all, and that deserves some recognition and thanks.

The same goes for the people on our planet. There are always people we are inspired by, whether that's a celebrity, a speaker, a musician or an activist. It's perfectly okay to be thankful for these people who we don't know personally, but who have added something to our lives in some way. Through great actors, we get great films, which we can enjoy in our own homes and get some much-needed downtime. Our favorite bands create songs that provide an audio backdrop to our memories. If you find yourself getting caught up in the negative news about the world, take some time to write your own headlines. Focus on what's great about the world we live in and the people in it. This can help to give some perspective on your life and make you feel thankful, rather than lacking in hope.

Remember your happy places

On your travels around the world, or even within your own city or town, there will always be places you come across that you feel connected to. When you are in such a place, take the time to look around and concentrate on what you can see, hear and feel.

You could create a journal of these happy places that you can look back on, and feel grateful that these wonderful bubbles exist in your world.

Keep me inspired

Write about three people in the world who inspire you

1 ....

....

....

....

2 ....

....

....

....

3 ....

....

....

....

Seek out good news

If you are struggling to focus on the good in the world, seek out happier stories. There are other sources out there that highlight heart-warming and inspiring news from around the world. Look at *goodnewsnetwork.org* for example, or set up a subscription to *thehappynewspaper.com*. Both will give you plenty to be thankful for in the world.

The places I've seen

Write about some of your favorite places in the world

....

....

....

....

....

....

Bless this planet

Give a few reasons why you're grateful for the planet we live on

....

....

....

....

....

....

....

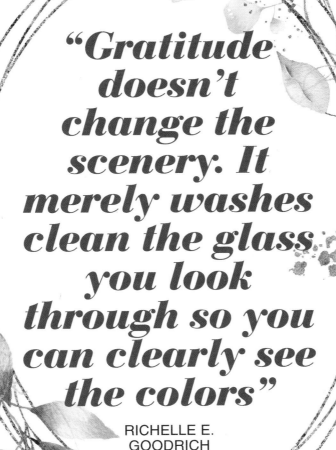

"Gratitude doesn't change the scenery. It merely washes clean the glass you look through so you can clearly see the colors"

RICHELLE E.
GOODRICH

Your working life

Work can take up so much of our lives, so why not make it a positive experience that you can feel grateful for every day?

For most of us, work takes up a large proportion of our week. If you don't like your job or it makes you feel overwhelmed and stressed, that's an awful lot of your time that is being taken up feeling negative. Practicing gratitude toward your career could be the change you need to get more out of your days and improve your overall well-being and stress levels.

"Gratitude can transform common days into thanksgivings, turn routine jobs into joy, and change ordinary opportunities into blessings"

WILLIAM ARTHUR WARD

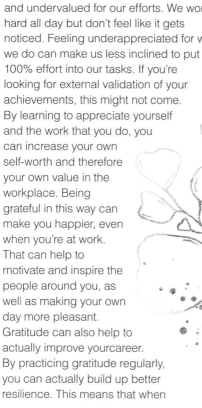

One of the biggest problems that we can have in these busy, modern, working lives we lead, is that we feel under-recognized and undervalued for our efforts. We work hard all day but don't feel like it gets noticed. Feeling underappreciated for what we do can make us less inclined to put 100% effort into our tasks. If you're looking for external validation of your achievements, this might not come. By learning to appreciate yourself and the work that you do, you can increase your own self-worth and therefore your own value in the workplace. Being grateful in this way can make you happier, even when you're at work. That can help to motivate and inspire the people around you, as well as making your own day more pleasant. Gratitude can also help to actually improve yourcareer. By practicing gratitude regularly, you can actually build up better resilience. This means that when something does go wrong at work, for example, you are better equipped to deal with it, rectify it and move on. It also helps you to focus on the things you actually do enjoy about your job, rather than the parts that make you feel overwhelmed. As well as our current career, we can also show gratitude toward our education. The things we learned as children in school, for example, are all skills that have brought us to where we are today. From learning to read to basic math, we're lucky to have had the opportunity to start life off in the right way. No matter where your educational path took you, or how long you were at school/college/university for, every day you turned up and learned has contributed to the person you are today. Plus, we have the opportunity to continue learning throughout our lives, if we want to, taking training courses or aspiring toward new qualifications.

Every job matters

Sometimes we might feel the job we have "isn't good enough," especially if we compare ourselves to others. But every job has its place in the world and makes a contribution to society. It's all about how you frame the job in your mind. Let's take, for example, a custodian in a hospital – think about how that custodian is creating a safe, hygienic environment for the patients who are recovering from illness or injury. It's a very important part of the medical system, and the role is essential. Try to focus on who you are helping with your job, and be thankful that your role enables you to do that.

The joys of work

What are five things that you love about your job?

1 ....
....

2 ....
....

3 ....
....

4 ....
....

5 ....
....

Give yourself an appraisal

Don't wait for a formal work review to get credit for all of your hard work. Grab your journal once a month and write down everything you have achieved at work in the previous few weeks. It doesn't always have to be the big stuff either, such as landing a new client or turning in a great report (though you should definitely include those!). Sometimes it can be as simple as finishing all your work for the day on time, clearing your email inbox, or helping a colleague in need.

School days

What are some of the most important things you learned at
school that help you in your life now?

....

....

....

....

....

....

....

Hard work pays off

What makes you good at your current job?

....

....

....

....

....

....

....

Maximize your leisure time

Our hobbies and interests help us to make the most of our leisure time, reduce stress and improve our overall well-being

Most of us have a hobby, whether we acknowledge that or not. Hobbies are often thought of as specific activities that we undertake. However, the definition of a hobby is "an activity done regularly in one's leisure time for pleasure." What do you do when you have time to yourself? You might indulge in something physical, like walking, yoga, swimming, running or going to the gym; something creative like painting, writing, scrapbooking, playing an instrument or taking photos; something mindful, like a puzzle or reading a book, cooking or baking; or a more niche activity like curating a collection of coins or bird watching. The scope of a hobby is very wide and it is unique to us as individuals. If you enjoy doing something and you do it on a regular basis, it's a hobby.

Maybe you haven't found the perfect hobby yet, but you would like to have something to enjoy in your leisure time. There is no one telling you what you can and can't try, and there is no one saying that you have to stick with a hobby you no longer enjoy. Hobbies change throughout our lives, as we grow older and our lives take different twists and turns. Priorities adapt and we might find we have less time to do the things we love. It's important to make time for these hobbies, as they bring us joy. Even if you can only fit in an hour a

Make time for yourself

Everyone needs time to do what they enjoy. It's easy to make excuses and find other things that need doing. But if you're choosing the housework over a hobby every time, you're neglecting the chance to bring a little more joy to your day. No matter how small a window, make time for your interests every day and do something you love. Be grateful for the opportunity to indulge in those things that make you happy and that you enjoy. It can help you to relax and make you more productive for the rest of your day.

week, you can be thankful for that hour, rather than fixating on how much time you wish you had to do what you love.

If you don't have a specific hobby, then there are other things that bring happiness to your leisure time. You might enjoy listening to music for example – you don't need to carve out specific time for that. You can use your commute to listen to tunes that lift your mood. Or maybe you find real joy in mindfully preparing and eating food – the simple pleasure of a perfectly ripe strawberry while sitting in the garden relaxing can really make you feel thankful for nature's bounty.

Busy as a bee

Write about some of your favorite hobbies and activities

....

....

....

....

....

....

....

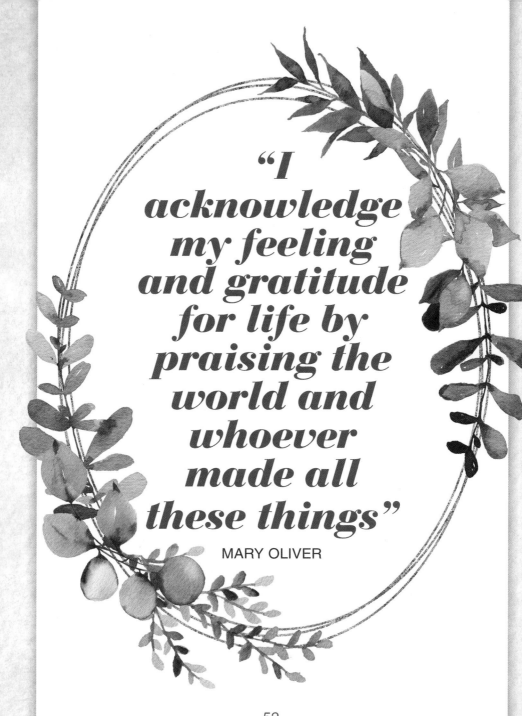

"I acknowledge my feeling and gratitude for life by praising the world and whoever made all these things"

MARY OLIVER

Pop cultured

What are some of the films, music, books or video games you are grateful for?

....

....

....

....

....

....

Share your interests

Having a hobby or interest doesn't have to be a solo activity – you can share your interests with those around you. For example, if you find baking an enjoyable hobby, why not invite a partner or child to help you and make it a connective experience? Or if you like to read, recommend your favorite book to a friend so that they can get the same joy out of it that you experienced when you read it.

Happy tummy

List your five favorite things to eat

1 ....

2 ....

3 ....

4 ....

5 ....

Journal

Your gratitude journal is exactly that – it's yours. The introduction on the next page suggests how you might choose to write your journal entries, but ultimately it's up to you to find a way that works best for you.

Your journal

Use your journal in whatever way feels natural to you,
whether you want to write in it every day or just occasionally –
it's your journal and there are no rules

O ver the following pages, you'll find a mixture of creative spaces and fun activities that, if you're open to it, will encourage you to develop your understanding and appreciation of exactly who you are. What's more, they will also help you to have more control over all aspects of your life in the future.

Each spread contains seven dedicated spaces where you can journal. One option could be to use one space for every day of the week. Many find this practice therapeutic, especially when it comes to letting go of things or making sense of the things that happen to us. Alternatively, if once a day is too much pressure, why not use one space per week? You could just use it at random when the occasion arises if you like, because that's the great thing about this practice – there are no hard and fast rules. Use the space as you see fit to improve whatever it is you want to work on, be it emotions, trauma, anxiety, stress or self improvement, or even if you're just using your journal as somewhere to make sense of it all. Furthermore, don't feel as though you have to write only about things that are happening in your life – you could write wishlists, or a plan for something you want to achieve; you could write in poetry form or a rap, or even just doodle. Use the space as you desire – this is your journal, after all.

You'll notice some prompts along the way. For example, you can keep a record of all the nice surprises or random acts of kindness you encounter in the "Unexpected" boxes; express who you feel gratitude toward in the "People" boxes; and use the "Notes" section as a complete blank canvas.

After every four journal spreads, you'll find some inspirational activities that walk you through a series of creatively stimulating tasks with a more thoughtful mindset, helping you to appreciate what you have and what you are capable of achieving. So, what are you waiting for? Dive in and enjoy the experience!

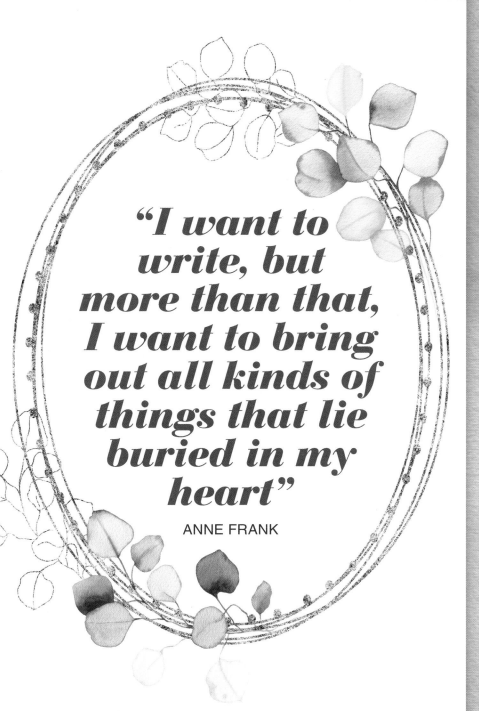

> "I want to write, but more than that, I want to bring out all kinds of things that lie buried in my heart"

ANNE FRANK

Week beginning

□□ · □□ · □□

1

2

3

4

5

6

7

"As we express our gratitude, we must never forget that the highest appreciation is not to utter words, but to live by them"

JOHN F. KENNEDY

Unexpected

Write down any pleasant surprises you've had this week

....

....

....

....

....

Notes ....

....

....

....

....

People

Who have you appreciated
this week and why?

....

....

....

....

....

....

....

....

....

□□·□□·□□

1

4

2

5

3

6

Live for now

Try to stay in the moment, rather than dwelling on the past or worrying about the future. Focus on the world around you and what you are doing now, which will help you to see all the positives in your current situation.

7

Unexpected

Write down any pleasant surprises you've had this week

....

....

....

....

....

Notes ....

....

....

....

....

....

....

....

....

....

....

People

Who have you appreciated
this week and why?

....

....

....

....

....

Week beginning

☐☐ · ☐☐ · ☐☐

1
....
....
....
....

> *"Gratitude is not only the greatest of virtues but the parent of all others"*
>
> **MARCUS TULLIUS CICERO**

2
....
....
....
....

5
....
....
....
....

3
....
....
....
....

6
....
....
....
....

4
....
....
....
....

7
....
....
....
....

Unexpected

Write down any pleasant surprises you've had this week

Notes

People

Who have you appreciated
this week and why?

1 ....

....

....

....

2 ....

....

....

....

3 ....

....

....

....

4 ....

....

....

....

5 ....

....

....

....

6 ....

....

....

....

7 ....

....

....

....

Make reminders

To enable gratitude to become a daily habit, leave little reminders. This could be sticky notes on the mirror or alerts that pop up on your phone. These should be prompts to reflect on what you are grateful for right now.

Unexpected

Write down any pleasant surprises you've had this week

....

....

....

....

....

Notes ....

....

....

....

....

....

....

....

....

....

....

....

People

Who have you appreciated
this week and why?

....

....

....

....

....

Writing a thank-you letter

Finding the words to thank someone face to face isn't always easy, which is why many turn to pen and paper (or keypad and screen) to express their feelings of gratitude, respect and love

Why we should thank people

It's all too easy to take the people in our lives for granted – it's natural human behavior, but the result can sometimes be quite hurtful. The best way to instantly right this wrong is to show that person your gratitude. By expressing your thanks and explaining just how grateful you are, you will make them feel appreciated and respected, helping you to sustain a happy relationship with them and absolve any residual feelings of guilt.

Preparing to write a letter

When preparing to write a gratitude letter, it's important not to put any pressure on yourself. Take the time to create a calm, safe space where you can write openly and honestly about your feelings. Some find a quiet environment aids concentration, while others prefer to use music to inspire emotion. Turning your phone off will help you to avoid distractions and get the job done. Remember you can always redraft, or go back to it later.

"Feeling gratitude and not expressing it is like wrapping a present and not giving it"

WILLIAM ARTHUR WARD

What to say

If you're struggling for inspiration, imagine the person you are writing to is no longer in your life – what would you miss about them, what do you wish you'd said when you had the opportunity, what have they done for you that has made an impact on your life or the person you are today? To help you get started, begin by putting together a list of ten "thank yous," or make a brainstorm.

What not to say

There are no right or wrong things to say here, but trying to keep things positive will help to keep you on track. If the person has wronged you or there are feelings of friction or frustration, try to turn those negative emotions into positive ones, by focusing on the things you would like to thank that person for. Remember no one is perfect, neither should they be made to feel that they ought to be.

Other ways to say thank you

While expressing your gratitude through words in the form of a thank-you letter will work for many people, it won't be the medium of choice for everyone. Other ways to express your thanks could take the form of a painting, a song, a cake, or even a video message. As long as you say it with love, it shouldn't matter how you say it.

My recipients

Write down the people you'd like to write a letter to

....

....

....

....

....

....

1

> *"Piglet noticed that even though he had a Very Small Heart, it could hold a rather large amount of Gratitude"*
>
> **A. A. MILNE**

2

5

3

6

4

7

Unexpected

Write down any pleasant surprises you've had this week

....

....

....

....

....

Notes ....

....

....

....

....

....

....

....

....

....

....

People

Who have you appreciated
this week and why?

....

....

....

....

....

Week beginning

□□ · □□ · □□

1

4

2

5

3

6

Save quotes

If you see a quote that you love, save it somewhere for future reference. This could be a quotes journal that you write down in, or you could start a Pinterest board. This will be a source of future inspiration.

7

Unexpected

Write down any pleasant surprises you've had this week

....

....

....

....

....

Notes ....

....

....

....

....

....

....

....

....

....

....

People

Who have you appreciated
this week and why?

....

....

....

....

....

1 _____

2 _____

3 _____

4 _____

5 _____

6 _____

7 _____

"The struggle ends when the gratitude begins"

NEALE DONALD WALSH

Unexpected

Write down any pleasant surprises you've had this week

....

....

....

....

....

Notes ....

....

....

....

....

....

People

Who have you appreciated
this week and why?

....

....

....

....

....

....

....

....

....

Week beginning

☐☐ · ☐☐ · ☐☐

1 ....
....
....
....
....

Gratitude boards

Create your own gratitude board at home, rather like a mood board. Use it to collect photos, quotes, tickets, memories and poems, for example, that showcase everything you have to be grateful for in one place.

2 ....
....
....
....

5 ....
....
....
....

3 ....
....
....
....

6 ....
....
....
....

4 ....
....
....
....

7 ....
....
....
....

Unexpected

Write down any pleasant surprises you've had this week

....

....

....

....

....

Notes ....

....

....

....

....

....

....

People

Who have you appreciated
this week and why?

....

....

....

....

....

....

....

....

....

Why we should all reconnect with nature

Technological advances can mean we spend less time outdoors, but here's how you can aid your connection to nature and reduce screen time

Human beings are hardwired to love nature and the vastness of the great outdoors. We all have our own personal reasons why we love being among the natural world. One of the most common reasons is the scientific link to greater psychological well-being, which is why we should be more grateful than ever for our connection to it.

Walk

Walking outside among nature is a wonderful way to reconnect to the healing power of the great outdoors. When was the last time you took a walk outside without any distractions? Without the need for a phone or music to distract you? Try to walk with purpose and take note of all the smells and beauty around you.

Bring nature indoors

If you live in an urban area, it can sometimes be hard to connect with nature – especially if you don't have access to a garden. So why not bring the natural world indoors with some houseplants? Not only do houseplants brighten up a room but they also improve air quality.

Look after the animals in your garden

As sentient beings, we have a responsibility to safeguard some of our most vulnerable species. Why not build a bat house for our flying nocturnal friends? Or make some seed balls for the birds to feed off in the cold winter months? These small gestures show your gratitude to all of the species that we share our wonderful planet with.

Play in the dirt

Bring out the inner child in you and get your hands and feet dirty every once in a while. This might mean immersing yourself in some gardening and feeling the vegetation against your skin. Or it could mean walking barefoot along the beach and feeling the rough uneven surfaces on the soles of your feet.

"Nature's beauty is a gift that cultivates appreciation and gratitude"
LOUIE SCHWARTZBERG

Get outside

I went for a walk today and I noticed...

Week beginning

□□ · □□ · □□

1 ....

....

....

....

2 ....

....

....

....

3 ....

....

....

....

4 ....

....

....

....

5 ....

....

....

....

6 ....

....

....

....

7 ....

....

....

....

"Appreciation can make a day – even change a life. Your willingness to put it into words is all that is necessary"

MARGARET COUSINS

Unexpected

Write down any pleasant surprises you've had this week

....

....

....

....

Notes ....

....

....

....

....

....

....

....

....

....

....

....

People

Who have you appreciated
this week and why?

....

....

....

....

....

1

2

3

4

5

6

Notice negativity

It's impossible to be positive all the time, but when you do have negative thoughts, don't push them away. Notice them, acknowledge them, feel them. Then, try to reframe them by looking for a positive aspect or approach.

7

Unexpected

Write down any pleasant surprises you've had this week

....

....

....

....

....

Notes ....

....

....

....

....

....

....

People

Who have you appreciated
this week and why?

....

....

....

....

....

....

....

....

....

Week beginning

☐☐ · ☐☐ · ☐☐

1

> *"If you are really thankful, what do you do? You share"*
>
> **W. CLEMENT STONE**

2

5

3

6

4

7

Unexpected

Write down any pleasant surprises you've had this week

....

....

....

....

....

Notes ....

....

....

....

....

....

....

People

Who have you appreciated
this week and why?

....

....

....

....

....

....

....

....

....

Week beginning

☐☐ · ☐☐ · ☐☐

1

2

3

4

5

6

7

Do not compare

Our attempts at gratitude can be disrupted if we're constantly comparing ourselves to others. You're on your own journey in life, so focus your thankfulness on your individual circumstances. Think about what you have and not what others have.

Unexpected

Write down any pleasant surprises you've had this week

....

....

....

....

Notes ....

....

....

....

....

....

....

People

Who have you appreciated
this week and why?

....

....

....

....

....

....

....

....

Find gratitude in creativity

Creative pursuits can push you to try something new, which boosts positivity and leads to feelings of happiness and ultimately being aware of, and grateful for, all that you have and are

You don't have to be an artist to be artistic, and you don't need to be a "creative" to be creative. There's no prescribed method – just do whatever makes you feel inspired. As well as reducing stress, creative activities can be challenging in a positive way, providing a much-needed boost of enthusiasm.

"Gratitude opens the door to the power, the wisdom, the creativity of the universe. You open the door through gratitude"

DEEPAK CHOPRA

Creative writing

Creative writing is a fantastically cathartic medium for vocalizing your gratitude. The key is to concentrate on a subject or theme that excites and interests you. However, if the thought of writing your first novel of 80,000 words is a tad overwhelming, start with poetry, short stories or even song writing to help to get those all-important creative juices flowing.

Scrapbooking

Scrapbooking is the beautiful art of preserving, presenting and arranging personal and family history – typically in the form of a book. It can be a very therapeutic way of organizing and appreciating your life's events, with photos, journal entries and memorabilia. Some parents prefer scrapbooking to keeping a "baby book" for their children, as it offers a literal and conceptual "blank canvas" to curate the items and events that are so important to you and your child.

Drawing

Drawing from your imagination, or letting it roam while doodling, is a good way to free your subconscious and find out what you're truly grateful for. Alternatively, focus on a particular scene or object from real life. By narrowing in on the task, other thoughts become quiet, leaving you free to rejoice in appreciation for other things.

Montaging

Montaging is making one large piece of art from several, smaller pieces. You could cut up and place together multiple photographs or postcards to remind you of your favorite people and places. Alternatively, why not create a film montage, using software to edit your favorite home movies together?

Gratitude tree

The idea behind a gratitude tree is that every time you feel grateful for something, you write it on a leaf and add it to the tree, which then becomes a piece of "living" art. This could be a 3D model or structure, or a growing mural on a wall. You could even invite family members or dinner guests to add to it whenever the occasion arises.

Week beginning

□□ · □□ · □□

1
....
....
....
....
....

> *"There may be reasons why we ought to be thankful for even those dispensations which appear dark and frowning"*
> **ALBERT BARNES**

2
....
....
....
....

5
....
....
....
....

3
....
....
....
....

6
....
....
....
....

4
....
....
....

7
....
....
....

Unexpected

Write down any pleasant surprises you've had this week

....

....

....

....

Notes ....

....

....

....

....

....

....

People

Who have you appreciated
this week and why?

....

....

....

....

....

....

....

....

1

2

3

4

5

6

7

Speak wisely

Thinking before you speak gives you a brief moment to compose your thoughts. Sometimes we speak rashly and don't fully comprehend our situation; a simple pause can give you time to choose your words carefully.

Unexpected

Write down any pleasant surprises you've had this week

....

....

....

....

....

Notes ....

....

....

....

....

....

People

Who have you appreciated
this week and why?

....

....

....

....

....

....

....

....

....

Week beginning

□□ · □□ · □□

1

5

2

6

3

7

4

> *"I'm thankful for each and every day. We never know when time is up"*
>
> **CHUCK BERRY**

Unexpected

Write down any pleasant surprises you've had this week

....

....

....

....

....

Notes ....

....

....

....

....

....

....

....

....

....

....

....

....

People

Who have you appreciated
this week and why?

....

....

....

....

....

1

Positive language

When speaking, whether that's to a partner, relative, friend or colleague, try to use words that are positive and uplifting. This can, in turn, make the person/people you're speaking to feel positive, too, even if you're tackling a difficult subject.

2

5

3

6

4

7

Unexpected

Write down any pleasant surprises you've had this week

....

....

....

....

....

Notes ....

....

....

....

....

....

....

People

Who have you appreciated
this week and why?

....

....

....

....

....

....

....

....

....

Make peace with your thoughts through meditation

In the modern world, our minds are constantly being stimulated, overworked and put under immense pressure. This is why it's more important than ever that we learn how to switch off our thoughts from time to time

The practice of meditation isn't necessarily the easiest hobby, but it's one that's well worth setting aside the time for. There are various types of meditation that can encourage you to find stillness in the mind, but you may find that some suit you better than others. Give these ones a go, and make a note of how each one works for you.

Guided

If you're new to meditation, this is probably a good place to start. Guided meditation involves the use of somebody talking you through the practice and inviting you to slowly begin switching off. This can be in the form of a class, an at-home video or an app like Headspace.

My experience: /10
Will you try this again? Yes / No

....

....

....

Transcendental

This type of meditation involves being seated and uses Sanskrit or mantras. The use of a mantra can help you to direct your focus and attention on a single word or phrase that is of importance to you. Whenever you find your mind wandering, you can come back to your mantra to recenter.

My experience: /10
Will you try this again? Yes / No

....

....

....

Mindfulness

Originating from Buddhist teachings, this is the most popular technique in the West. Mindfulness meditation involves the practitioner paying attention to their thoughts while simultaneously allowing them to pass them by without judgement. This is a common type of meditation that can be practiced at home without a teacher. Try visualising each thought as a cloud that passes you by.

My experience: /10
Will you try this again? Yes / No

....
....
....

Movement

There is nothing to suggest that meditation has to solely involve sitting still. You can also find the same stillness internally through gentle movement of the body. This can be anything from a gentle yoga class to a walk among nature. If you choose the latter, try to avoid any distraction from technology, and walk in total silence.

My experience: /10
Will you try this again? Yes / No

....
....
....

Spiritual

Used in Eastern cultures and religions, including Buddhism and Hinduism, this practice is ideal if you are keen to develop more of a spiritual awakening. This style of meditation becomes more of a prayer, and provides you with a gateway to God, a specific deity or the universe. If you are keen to embark on a spiritual journey, you could try using certain essential oils and scents to heighten your experience. These can include frankincense or palo santo.

My experience: /10
Will you try this again? Yes / No

....
....
....

Week beginning

□□ · □□ · □□

1 ....
....
....
....

2 ....
....
....
....

3 ....
....
....
....

4 ....
....
....
....

5 ....
....
....
....

6 ....
....
....
....

7 ....
....
....
....

"Gratitude is when memory is stored in the heart and not in the mind"

LIONEL HAMPTON

Unexpected

Write down any pleasant surprises you've had this week

....

....

....

....

....

Notes ....

....

....

....

....

....

....

People

Who have you appreciated
this week and why?

....

....

....

....

....

....

....

....

....

Week beginning

□□·□□·□□

1

4

2

5

3

6

Appreciate everything

When you start to appreciate even the smallest of things, you will bring more joy to your life. Don't take anything for granted, even if it's as simple as a hot cup of tea or your favorite show on TV.

7

Unexpected

Write down any pleasant surprises you've had this week

....

....

....

....

....

Notes ....

....

....

....

....

....

....

People

Who have you appreciated
this week and why?

....

....

....

....

....

....

....

....

....

Week beginning

☐☐ · ☐☐ · ☐☐

1

2

3

4

5

6

7

> *"We often take for granted the very things that most deserve our gratitude"*
>
> **CYNTHIA OZICK**

Unexpected

Write down any pleasant surprises you've had this week

....

....

....

....

....

Notes

....

....

....

....

....

....

....

....

....

....

People

Who have you appreciated
this week and why?

....

....

....

....

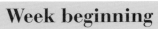
1 ....

....

....

....

2 ....

....

....

....

3 ....

....

....

....

....

4 ....

....

....

....

5 ....

....

....

....

6 ....

....

....

....

7 ....

....

....

....

Mindful
social media

If you use social media wisely, it
can connect you to things happening
in your community, local charities you
can support, or a way to stay in
contact with friends – curate your
feed to be a positive place.

Unexpected

Write down any pleasant surprises you've had this week

....

....

....

....

....

Notes ....

....

....

....

....

....

....

....

....

....

People

Who have you appreciated
this week and why?

....

....

....

....

....

It's cool to be kind

Helping others not only offers perspective on our own lives, but it also enriches our souls by making us feel positive and purposeful

R andom acts of kindness don't need to be huge statements – they are simply small gestures of goodwill to another living being that leaves us feeling happy and euphoric. Have you ever offered to pay for someone's shopping when they've left their wallet at home, or taken the trash out for an elderly neighbor? Or maybe you've taken part in a five-minute beach clean. These all count as random acts of kindness, and no matter how big or small, they all help to restore our faith in humanity.

All for one, one for all

Make a list of some of the random acts of kindness you've carried out

....

....

....

....

....

....

....

....

Litter pick

Grab some gardening gloves, a trash bag and a litter picker, and get yourself down to your local park or beach for a litter pick. It's amazing how much you can pick up in just a short stroll. It will feel good to know you're not only increasing the beauty of the area, but you'll also be safeguarding the creatures that inhabit it too.

Buy food for a homeless person

There is currently an epidemic of homeless people on our streets. Even though you might think you can't help, there are small gestures that can be the difference between a good or a bad day. So, next time you pass a homeless person, consider taking a minute to ask them what they'd like to eat if you feel it's safe to do so, and offer them a tasty treat.

Help out in your local soup kitchen

Most towns have a soup kitchen that runs most evenings. These charities provide homeless people with a hot meal and they're often in need of volunteers. Even offering one evening a every two weeks can make a difference. Seeing people with nothing can often make us look at our own lives and feel grateful for what we have.

Love thy neighbor

Make a list of random acts of kindness people have shown you

....

....

....

....

....

....

Week beginning

☐☐ · ☐☐ · ☐☐

1 ....
....
....
....

> "There is a calmness to a life lived in gratitude, a quiet joy"
>
> **RALPH H. BLUM**

2 ....
....
....
....

5 ....
....
....
....

3 ....
....
....
....

6 ....
....
....
....

4 ....
....
....
....

7 ....
....
....
....

Unexpected

Write down any pleasant surprises you've had this week

....

....

....

....

....

Notes ....

....

....

....

....

....

People

Who have you appreciated
this week and why?

....

....

....

....

....

....

....

....

....

1

4

2

5

3

6

Reframe
the negatives

Try to look for things to be grateful
for in negative situations. It can be
incredibly hard sometimes, but if
you can find a silver lining or a small
spark of hope, it can help you to
face difficult times.

7

Unexpected

Write down any pleasant surprises you've had this week

....

....

....

....

....

Notes ....

....

....

....

....

....

....

....

....

....

....

People

Who have you appreciated
this week and why?

....

....

....

....

Week beginning

☐☐ · ☐☐ · ☐☐

1

2

3

4

5

6

7

> "I still miss those I loved who are no longer with me, but I find I am grateful for having loved them. The gratitude has finally conquered the loss"
>
> **RITA MAE BROWN**

Unexpected

Write down any pleasant surprises you've had this week

....

....

....

....

Notes

....

....

....

....

....

....

....

....

....

....

....

....

People

Who have you appreciated
this week and why?

....

....

....

....

1 ....
....
....
....
....

Practice mindfulness

Mindfulness and gratitude go hand in hand. When you free up your mind to focus on what is right in front of you, you see more things to be grateful for. Try to set aside time every day for a mindful practice.

2 ....
....
....
....

5 ....
....
....
....

3 ....
....
....
....

6 ....
....
....
....

4 ....
....
....
....

7 ....
....
....
....

Unexpected

Write down any pleasant surprises you've had this week

....

....

....

....

....

Notes ....

....

....

....

....

....

People

Who have you appreciated
this week and why?

....

....

....

....

....

....

....

....

....

Appreciate good food & drink

There's so much to be thankful for when it comes to food –
not only is it fuel for survival, but cooking it can inspire passion
and eating it brings plenty of pleasure

Cooking doesn't have to be a chore; use it as an opportunity for mindfulness – the practice of being in the moment to appreciate the bounty before you. So think about the sound the knife makes as it slices through an onion, lose yourself in the motion as you use a spoon to swirl a sauce, and consider what words come to mind as you take that ever-so-satisfying first bite.

Healthy eating and its benefits

While eating "junk" foods can make us feel happy, the sensation is short-lived and the health complications that can arise from regularly consuming "bad" food can last a lifetime. The key is to enjoy "treats" in moderation, and find ways to appreciate nutritious food instead, which will give you plenty of things to be thankful for, including a more positive outlook, healthier skin, better sleep and more energy.

Grow your own

People who grow their own food say the taste and feeling of reward is nothing like you achieve from store-bought goods, not to mention it sparks an appreciation for Mother Nature. The best part about growing your own fruit and veg is that it isn't complicated – soil, seeds, sun and water are pretty much all it takes. Some of the easiest food to get started with includes lettuce, potatoes, peas, beans (fava and lima), onions, garlic and tomatoes.

Garden to table

List some fruits and vegetables that you could grow and when you'd need to plant them

....

....

....

Spice of life

What spices are essential to
your style of cooking?

- ....

- ....

- ....

- ....

Good to go

Think of a few healthy and delicious
smoothie ideas you could try out

- ....

- ....

- ....

- ....

Try something new

List a few new meals you would like to try over the next week or so

....

....

....

....

....

Week beginning

☐☐ · ☐☐ · ☐☐

1

2

3

4

5

6

7

"Reflect upon your present blessings, of which every man has plenty; not on your past misfortunes of which all men have some"

CHARLES DICKENS

Unexpected

Write down any pleasant surprises you've had this week

....

....

....

....

....

Notes ....

....

....

....

....

....

....

....

....

....

People

Who have you appreciated
this week and why?

....

....

....

....

....

1 ....

2 ....

3 ....

4 ....

5 ....

6 ....

7 ....

Gratitude as habit

Like everything, the more you practice something, the more it becomes a habit. Make writing in your gratitude journal part of your bedtime routine, at the same time every day. It will then become a habit of little effort.

Unexpected

Write down any pleasant surprises you've had this week

....

....

....

....

....

Notes ....

....

....

....

....

....

....

People

Who have you appreciated
this week and why?

....

....

....

....

....

....

....

....

....

Week beginning

□□ · □□ · □□

1

> "Silent gratitude isn't much use to anyone"
>
> G. B. STERN

2

5

3

6

4

7

Unexpected

Write down any pleasant surprises you've had this week

....

....

....

....

....

Notes ....

....

....

....

....

....

....

People

Who have you appreciated
this week and why?

....

....

....

....

....

....

....

....

....

1

2

3

4

5

6

7

Read your journal

Writing down what you're grateful for is the best way to cement gratitude in your life. Writing something down can make it feel more "real." Look back when times are hard to remind yourself of the good in your life.

Unexpected

Write down any pleasant surprises you've had this week

Notes

People

Who have you appreciated
this week and why?

The power of music

Music can carry you away out of yourself or help you to delve into your innermost thoughts and feelings – it has a power like nothing else

Music is an invisible force that weaves its way into our minds, helping us to find ourselves, affect our feelings, alter our mood, inspire emotion, and alleviate stress. Music can lift us up, bring us down, help us to unwind or help us to feel energized – that is the versatile magic of music.

Live music

If listening to music via your headphones is level 1, seeing your favorite band or singer perform live is level 100. Alongside the music itself, the artists offer a tangible performance, with human interaction that creates an uplifting atmosphere that only a select number of people will witness in real time. Furthermore, the performers will most likely vocalize their appreciation of your support, which leads you to feel valued, thus continuing the upward spiral of positive emotion.

Live and in person

What was the first gig you went to?

....

What was the last gig you went to?

....

Who is the best live performer you've ever seen?

....

Mood-altering music

When you listen to a song that excites you, the brain releases dopamine, the feel-good chemical, which is why you are inclined to want to listen again. The same is true of sad songs, which scientists say release the hormone prolactin, a chemical that curbs grief.

"One good thing about music: when it hits you, you feel no pain"

BOB MARLEY

Significant songs

Listening to music can move you in all manner of ways. The reason some songs are more significant to you than others is said to be linked to memories and early childhood influences. There could be a hook in the melody that is reminiscent of something your parents liked that you heard growing up, or particular lyrics might strike a chord with something that happened in your past or that you are currently going through now.

Lost in the rhythm

What is the most important song or piece of music to you and why?

....

....

How does it make you feel when you hear it?

....

....

What song cheers you up when you're feeling down?

....

What song will get you on the dancefloor?

....

What kind of music do you listen to when you're exercising?

....

Week beginning

☐☐ · ☐☐ · ☐☐

1 ....
....
....
....

> *"We can only be said to be alive in those moments when our hearts are conscious of our treasures"*
>
> **THORNTON WILDER**

2 ....
....
....
....

5 ....
....
....
....

3 ....
....
....
....

6 ....
....
....
....

4 ....
....
....
....

7 ....
....
....
....

Unexpected

Write down any pleasant surprises you've had this week

....

....

....

....

....

Notes ....

....

....

....

....

....

....

....

People

Who have you appreciated
this week and why?

....

....

....

....

....

....

....

....

....

....

□□ · □□ · □□

1

4

2

5

3

6

Spend time wisely

Choose who you spend your
time with very carefully. You
don't have endless free time, so
opt to spend it with people who you
simply love to be around,
who make you happy and who
bring you joy.

7

Unexpected

Write down any pleasant surprises you've had this week

....

....

....

....

....

Notes ....

....

....

....

....

....

People

Who have you appreciated
this week and why?

....

....

....

....

....

....

....

....

Week beginning

☐☐ · ☐☐ · ☐☐

1

2

3

4

5

6

7

> *"Gratitude is an antidote to negative emotions, a neutralizer of envy, hostility, worry, and irritation. It is savoring; it is not taking things for granted; it is present-oriented"*
>
> **SONJA LYUBOMIRSKY**

Unexpected

Write down any pleasant surprises you've had this week

....

....

....

....

....

Notes

....

....

....

....

....

....

....

....

....

....

People

Who have you appreciated
this week and why?

....

....

....

....

....

Week beginning

☐☐ · ☐☐ · ☐☐

1
....
....
....
....
....

Just three things

We know some days are harder than others, but try to commit to finding and writing down three things you are grateful for every day. They don't have to be big things – just the process can help you to feel better about your day.

2
....
....
....
....

5
....
....
....
....

3
....
....
....
....

6
....
....
....
....

4
....
....
....
....

7
....
....
....
....

Unexpected

Write down any pleasant surprises you've had this week

....

....

....

....

....

Notes ....

....

....

....

....

....

....

People

Who have you appreciated
this week and why?

....

....

....

....

....

....

....

....

....

Declutter for a better life

Decluttering your personal environment can help you to gain a sense of order, perspective and worth, not to mention it can give you a whole new appreciation for the items you keep

W e accumulate clutter without really being aware of it. It's only when literal space or our mental well-being become factors do we stop and assess what we truly need. Decluttering won't only improve your environment, but it will also help you to feel empowered, liberated and in control.

What is clutter?

A person's home should be their castle, not a hoarder's paradise, but if you have a "keep it/buy it just in case" mentality, your house could soon be filled with things you don't need, and in some instances it turns out you didn't really want after all. If it's broken, unwanted, not needed, outgrown or unloved, then it's clutter – you don't need it and it's time to give it away or get rid of it somehow.

How to declutter

Decluttering is a marathon, not a sprint. Take one room at a time, and within each room one area at a time. For example, a wardrobe, a set of kitchen cupboards, a toy box and so on. Put everything from that area in a pile in the center of the room. Hold each item in turn and consider the feeling it inspires. If it's positive, keep it. If it's negative or neutral, then you can do without it.

"Have gratitude for the things you're discarding. By giving gratitude, you're giving closure to the relationship with that object, and by doing so, it becomes a lot easier to let go"

MARIE KONDO

Sentimental items

The hardest items to let go of are sentimental ones, but if you're only keeping an item because you feel you ought to, rather than want to, it's time to let it go. Hold the object, thank it for the memories, and donate it.

Declutter your life

A calendar, in whatever form, is the most simple yet effective way to manage your time. A good trick is to color-block activities into groups (work, home, kids, gym, social life and so on), so you are instantly aware of how much time you devote to what. Take a good look, and decide where you can cut back on things that demand too much of you, and be sure to schedule in "recharge" events for some "me time."

Tidy space, tidy mind

What could you do to declutter your life?

....

....

....

....

....

....

....

....

Week beginning

□□ · □□ · □□

1

2

3

4

5

6

7

> "He is a wise man who does not grieve for the things which he has not, but rejoices for those which he has"
>
> **EPICTETUS**

Unexpected

Write down any pleasant surprises you've had this week

....

....

....

....

....

Notes ....

....

....

....

....

....

....

People

Who have you appreciated
this week and why?

....

....

....

....

....

....

....

....

....

....

Week beginning

□□ · □□ · □□

1

2

3

4

5

6

7

Family gratitude

Speak to your family about the importance of gratitude, and encourage them to join you in looking for the positives in the every day. Between you, you might come up with more than you would think of on your own.

Unexpected

Write down any pleasant surprises you've had this week

....

....

....

....

....

Notes ....

....

....

....

....

....

....

....

....

....

....

People

Who have you appreciated
this week and why?

....

....

....

....

Week beginning

☐☐ · ☐☐ · ☐☐

1 ....
....
....
....

> *"Enjoy the little things, for one day you may look back and realize they were the big thing"*
>
> **ROBERT BRAULT**

2 ....
....
....
....

3 ....
....
....
....

4 ....
....
....
....

5 ....
....
....
....

6 ....
....
....
....

7 ....
....
....
....

Unexpected

Write down any pleasant surprises you've had this week

....

....

....

....

....

Notes ....

....

....

....

....

....

....

People

Who have you appreciated
this week and why?

....

....

....

....

....

....

....

....

....

Week beginning

☐☐ · ☐☐ · ☐☐

1 ....

....

....

....

2 ....

....

....

....

3 ....

....

....

....

4 ....

....

....

....

5 ....

....

....

....

6 ....

....

....

....

7 ....

....

....

....

Thank
your partner

We can take the people in our
lives for granted. If you have a
partner, remember to show them
gratitude for what they do for you.
This applies to family members
and friends too. It will make them
feel loved.

Unexpected

Write down any pleasant surprises you've had this week

....

....

....

....

....

Notes ....

....

....

....

....

....

....

....

....

....

....

People

Who have you appreciated
this week and why?

....

....

....

....

....

Sleep your way happy

Getting enough good-quality sleep can have a huge impact on your well-being. When you're well rested, you're better able to appreciate your surroundings and environment

Sleep isn't a luxury. By getting enough restful sleep, you'll have more energy to face each day. You'll also have improved mental health and physical health, less risk of illness and better alertness. It can also help you to feel more in tune with the world and better able to notice the things around you.

Plan pre-bed activities

Rather than looking at your phone, think about what you can do instead before bedtime. If you want to read, put a book in plain sight, so it prompts you to pick it up. Or put a journal and pen next to your bed so you can write about your day.

"Happiness consists in getting enough sleep. Just that, nothing more"

ROBERT A. HEINLEIN

Banish the tech

Having tech and gadgets, such as phones or laptops, in your bedroom makes it tempting to use them before going to sleep. Remove chargers from your bedroom and create a charging station elsewhere. Decide on a time when you will put your tech on this station before going to bed, and leave it there until the morning.

Plan your bedtime routine

It's not just kids that benefit from a solid bedtime routine. It really helps us as adults too. Grab a notepad and pen and think about what your perfect bedtime routine would involve, whether this includes a warm bath, time to read a book, writing down thoughts in a gratitude journal or using a lavender pillow spray. Then, thinking about your ideal bedtime, work backward and assign times to these steps to create a routine you can follow.

Cleanse your sleep environment

If you want to sleep well, you have to create a haven that feels relaxing. Start by removing any clutter on surfaces in your bedroom. Consider whether your sheets are comfy and add a blanket to your bed if you get cold. Dim night lights can help you to relax, rather than bright overhead lights. Ensure your curtains block out light, and eliminate any other sources of light, such as LED clocks or lights on plug switches.

Counting sheep

On average, how many hours of sleep do you get a night?

....

What are a few things you can do to try to improve your quality of sleep?

....

....

....

Week beginning

☐☐ · ☐☐ · ☐☐

1

2

3

4

"Gratitude unlocks the fullness of life. It turns what we have into enough, and more"

MELODY BEATTIE

5

6

7

Unexpected

Write down any pleasant surprises you've had this week

....

....

....

....

....

Notes ....

....

....

....

....

....

....

People

Who have you appreciated
this week and why?

....

....

....

....

....

....

....

....

....

Week beginning

☐☐ · ☐☐ · ☐☐

1 ....

2 ....

3 ....

4 ....

5 ....

6 ....

7 ....

Thank yourself

We often focus all of our gratitude on external things and people, but remember to thank yourself too. Give yourself praise when you deserve it and acknowledge your achievements, and be thankful for your own health and well-being.

Unexpected

Write down any pleasant surprises you've had this week

....

....

....

....

....

Notes ....

....

....

....

....

....

....

....

....

....

....

....

People

Who have you appreciated
this week and why?

....

....

....

....

....

Week beginning

☐☐ · ☐☐ · ☐☐

1

2

3

4

5

6

7

"It's a funny thing about life, once you begin to take note of the things you are grateful for, you begin to lose sight of the things that you lack"

GERMANY KENT

Unexpected

Write down any pleasant surprises you've had this week

....

....

....

....

....

Notes ....

....

....

....

....

....

....

People

Who have you appreciated
this week and why?

....

....

....

....

....

....

....

....

....

1

Be a volunteer

Volunteer at your local charity shop, in the community, at a sports event, on a garden project, or something else. Volunteering in any way is shown to improve your own mental health and well-being, as well as promote feelings of gratitude.

2

5

3

6

4

7

Unexpected

Write down any pleasant surprises you've had this week

_____

_____

_____

_____

_____

Notes _____

_____

_____

_____

_____

_____

_____

People

Who have you appreciated
this week and why?

_____

_____

_____

_____

_____

_____

_____

_____

_____

Get in touch with your senses

Don't take your five senses for granted. Tap in to each of
them in turn to help you become more focused and
mindful toward the world around you

We use our key senses every day to see, hear, smell, taste and feel
our way around our environment. By paying attention to these
senses, we can become more in tune with the things around us and
in turn more grateful for what we have in our lives. Try these five simple activities
to stimulate your senses.

I spy...

"I spy" is not just for kids
(although they can join in too!).
Playing this simple game
forces you to really focus on
your surroundings. Challenge
yourself to find something for
every letter of the alphabet (or
your name), or work through
the colors of the rainbow.

Listen to your home

We take our homes for
granted and don't notice
everyday sounds. Take a
moment to sit down in a
comfortable spot and focus on
the sounds around you. This
might be passing traffic,
people talking in the street or
birds in the yard. Which noise
do you find the most
comforting?

Taste when you cook

If you're always rushing to
cook a quick meal, slow down
and engage your sense of
taste. When you're cooking
your next dish, make an effort
to taste the different ingredients
that you're adding individually.
How does this new taste
change the overall taste of your
meal? This will help you to
connect to what you're eating
in a more mindful way.

Get in touch with nature

Go for a walk in nature,
whether in a local park, on a
beach or in a forest. You might
be used to using your sense of
hearing to notice the sounds
around you, but why not
engage your sense of touch?
Explore the textures of the
natural world in a tactile way.
What does bark on a tree feel
like? How do leaves on trees
differ in texture? How does
sand between your toes feel?

Wake up and smell the flowers

Head out into your garden (or someone else's or your nearest green space) and use your nose. There are a lot of natural smells in nature that you might not notice when they're all mingled in together. Rub your fingers on different flowers and herbs, and see what they smell like. You'll find yourself drawn toward certain smells more than others – which ones appeal to you the most?

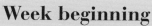

Week beginning

□□ · □□ · □□

1

2

3

4

5

6

7

"The purpose of life is to live it, to taste experience to the utmost, to reach out eagerly and without fear for newer and richer experience"

ELEANOR ROOSEVELT

Unexpected

Write down any pleasant surprises you've had this week

....

....

....

....

....

Notes ....

....

....

....

....

....

....

....

....

....

People

Who have you appreciated
this week and why?

....

....

....

....

....

....

1 ....

....

....

....

2 ....

....

....

....

3 ....

....

....

....

4 ....

....

....

....

5 ....

....

....

....

6 ....

....

....

....

7 ....

....

....

....

Send gratitude messages

Technology isn't going anywhere, so use it to do good. Send kind messages to friends and family if they're having a hard time, or just to say thank you to them. They will really appreciate it.

Unexpected

Write down any pleasant surprises you've had this week

Notes

People

Who have you appreciated
this week and why?

Week beginning

☐☐ · ☐☐ · ☐☐

1

2

3

4

> *"People who enjoy what they are doing invariably do it well"*
>
> **JOE GIBBS**

5

6

7

Unexpected

Write down any pleasant surprises you've had this week

....

....

....

....

....

Notes ....

....

....

....

....

....

....

People

Who have you appreciated
this week and why?

....

....

....

....

....

....

....

....

....

1

2

3

4

5

6

7

Bookend with gratitude

Try to start and finish your day with gratitude. Use the mornings to think about your upcoming day and focus on the things you're looking forward to, then at the end of the day reflect on what you are thankful for.

Unexpected

Write down any pleasant surprises you've had this week

....

....

....

....

....

Notes ....

....

....

....

....

....

....

People

Who have you appreciated
this week and why?

....

....

....

....

....

....

....

....

....

The power of moving more

We could all benefit from moving our bodies more, but it's time we started thinking outside the box and finding other fun ways to incorporate exercise into our day to day

Walking

Often when people think of exercise, they believe it needs to be physical endurance, but that's not the case. In fact, you can reap similar benefits just by taking a stroll around your local park, along the beach or to the corner shop. If you find yourself tight for time, why not park further away from work? Or jump off the bus a stop early? Incorporating walking into your morning routine is a great way to set you up for a day at work.

Wild swimming

Swimming itself is a great way to get fit, but have you ever thought about giving wild swimming a go? Wild swimming is for thrill-seekers, because it gives you a sense of adventure in the great outdoors. If you are looking to wild swim, then any footpath, footbridge or "open access" land that borders a lake or river is a great place to start. The number of health and physiological benefits of cold water immersion is endless, so give it a go!

"All truly great thoughts are conceived while walking"

FRIEDRICH NIETZSCHE

Gardening

It's not your average form of high-intensity exercise, but gardening is a great way to get you outside and moving. According to the American Heart Association, planting and weeding is considered "moderate exercise," which is great news if you already spend hours working on your veggie patch. It's also a well-known fact that spending time in nature directly impacts your mental well-being.

Surfing

Surfing requires a lot of stamina and strength, but you'll never regret zipping up your wetsuit and heading into the sea – even if it is for a bit of fun and to get splashed by the waves. Most of the power to push off on a wave comes from your upper body and core strength, making it a great way to tone your body. It will leave you feeling energized, invigorated and wanting more.

Running

One of the best things about running is how quickly you can begin to see your progress. The initial few runs might feel like hard work, but running is great because it doesn't require any commitment to a costly gym membership, and it enables you to get outside among nature. Going out for a jog also has excellent head-clearing benefits, as it reduces anxiety and stress.

Make it easy

Write down some simple ways you can move more in everyday life

....

....

....

....

....

Week beginning

☐☐ · ☐☐ · ☐☐

1 ....

"Slow down and enjoy life. It's not only the scenery you miss by going to fast – you also miss the sense of where you are going and why"

EDDIE CANTOR

2 ....

5 ....

3 ....

6 ....

4 ....

7 ....

Unexpected

Write down any pleasant surprises you've had this week

....

....

....

....

....

Notes ....

....

....

....

....

....

....

People

Who have you appreciated
this week and why?

....

....

....

....

....

....

....

....

Week beginning

□□ · □□ · □□

1 ....

4 ....

2 ....

5 ....

3 ....

6 ....

Enjoy nature

Get outside in nature as much as you can. Being connected with our environment can make us feel calmer, happier and more grateful. Carve out time to walk, run or cycle, focusing on the natural sounds and things you see.

7 ....

Unexpected

Write down any pleasant surprises you've had this week

Notes

People

Who have you appreciated this week and why?

Week beginning

□□ · □□ · □□

1 ....

2 ....

3 ....

4 ....

5 ....

6 ....

7 ....

> *"Thankfulness is the beginning of gratitude. Gratitude is the completion of thankfulness. Thankfulness may consist merely of words. Gratitude is shown in acts"*
>
> **HENRI FREDERIC AMIEL**

Unexpected

Write down any pleasant surprises you've had this week

....

....

....

....

....

Notes ....

....

....

....

....

....

....

....

....

....

....

People

Who have you appreciated
this week and why?

....

....

....

....

....

1 ....
....
....
....

Curate social media

Leave destructive social media if you need to. You can close accounts completely, or you can just choose to unfollow people or accounts that make you feel negative. No one is obliged to be online.

2 ....
....
....
....

5 ....
....
....
....

3 ....
....
....
....

6 ....
....
....
....

4 ....
....
....
....

7 ....
....
....
....

Unexpected

Write down any pleasant surprises you've had this week

....

....

....

....

....

Notes ....

....

....

....

....

....

....

People

Who have you appreciated
this week and why?

....

....

....

....

....

....

....

....

Making plans

Creating events, making plans and generally having nice things to look forward to helps to add fun punctuation marks in this merry old carousel we call life

Planning helps us to bring the future into the present, and by doing so gives us a feeling of control over our lives. None of us knows how long we have, so it's important to live life to the fullest – making plans and completing goals brings a meaning and validation that helps us to feel as though we have achieved that.

"If you want to live a happy life, tie it to a goal, not to people or things"
ALBERT EINSTEIN

How to make plans

Write down a list of things you want to achieve, such as: write a novel, swim with dolphins, be a space tourist, start your own business and so on. Next to each one, add reasons that are stopping you from completing them today, for example: time, money and so on. Now, next to each idea write down a plan of how you could achieve that goal, for example, for the novel: write a page a night; for swimming with dolphins: research destinations and start a savings plan.

How to ensure plans become reality

To achieve your "bucket list," give yourself a time frame. Post the list on your fridge and add an ideal completion date to each. Add regular reminders on your calendar to check in with yourself on how much progress you've made. You might find you can work toward several goals at once, just don't overload yourself.

Time for adventure

What would you like to learn?

....

....

....

Where would you like to visit?

....

....

....

What would you like to experience?

....

....

....

What goals would you like to achieve in the next five years?

....

....

....

....

....

Week beginning

☐☐·☐☐·☐☐

1

2

3

4

5

6

7

"Start each day with a positive thought and a grateful heart"

ROY T. BENNETT

Unexpected

Write down any pleasant surprises you've had this week

....

....

....

....

....

Notes ....

....

....

....

....

....

....

....

People

Who have you appreciated
this week and why?

....

....

....

....

....

....

....

....

....

Week beginning

☐☐ · ☐☐ · ☐☐

1

2

3

4

5

6

7

Enjoy your life

Try to enjoy what you have in your life right now. Things pass us by so quickly that we don't even notice them. For example, when you're going to work, take in all the sights and sounds for a more mindful experience.

Unexpected

Write down any pleasant surprises you've had this week

....

....

....

....

....

Notes

....

....

....

....

....

....

....

People

Who have you appreciated
this week and why?

....

....

....

....

....

....

....

....

....

....

Week beginning

☐☐ · ☐☐ · ☐☐

1

2

3

4

5

6

7

> *"The real gift of gratitude is that the more grateful you are, the more present you become"*
>
> **ROBERT HOLDEN**

Unexpected

Write down any pleasant surprises you've had this week

....

....

....

....

....

Notes ....

....

....

....

....

....

....

People

Who have you appreciated
this week and why?

....

....

....

....

....

....

....

....

....

....

1

2

3

4

5

6

7

Help other people

Helping others can make us feel more grateful in our own lives. Whether that's offering to do shopping for an older family member, or lending a listening ear to a friend, giving some time to others can certainly benefit your own well-being.

Unexpected

Write down any pleasant surprises you've had this week

....

....

....

....

....

Notes ....

....

....

....

....

....

....

....

....

....

People

Who have you appreciated
this week and why?

....

....

....

....

....

Learn something new

Life is full of moments that allow you to learn new things.
Big or small, every new piece of information or skill that you acquire makes
you a better, stronger version of yourself

Every day is a school day because our brains love to learn! Every time a new bit of knowledge is acquired, neurons are stimulated, which form more pathways in the brain that enable electrical impulses to travel faster. That's why practice really does make perfect! Beyond that, learning is achieving a goal, which releases endorphins, making you feel happier and better about yourself. What's not to love?

Skill

The great thing about learning a new skill is there are literally hundreds to choose from. Just close your eyes and think of something you've always wanted to try. How about public speaking, photography, how to salsa, how to play the piano, or learning self-defense. If time and money are against you, start with online tutorials that have good reviews, and try learning more every day.

Craft

There's nothing quite like that feeling you get when making something with your own two hands, and that's exactly what you get by learning a new craft. Knitting, baking, sewing, basket making… the list goes on. The great thing about crafts is that they can be done in bitesize projects, so you can learn to walk before you run, or candle-make, or quill, or whittle…

"Tell me and I forget. Teach me and I remember. Involve me and I learn"

BENJAMIN FRANKLIN

Language

There are thought to be approximately 6,500 spoken languages in the world, and it's estimated that half of the world's population only speak one. Speaking a foreign language not only improves your memory, communication skills and vacation options, but it also makes you more employable. There are plenty of online tutorials and apps that can help to get you started.

Sport

Exercise, in all its guises, is proven to boost both physical and mental health, and the great thing about sports is that there's something for everyone – young or old, fit or not. Once you decide on the sport you want to play, do an online search to find a team or fitness center in your area that offers it.

Qualification

Whether you're taking that next step on your career path or thinking of switching lanes, a new qualification improves your skillset, boosts your prospects, widens your network of contacts, and can give you a renewed sense of motivation. Head online for a wealth of knowledge, tips and options for finding a course and qualification that suits you.

An active mind

This time next year, what do you hope to have learned?

....

....

....

....

Your gratitude journey

You may have reached the end of this journal,
but your gratitude journey is just beginning

We are often encouraged to focus more of our attention on living in the present moment, rather than dwelling on past or future ties, commitments and memories. However, as you reach the final few pages of this gratitude journal, we welcome you to take a retrospective dive into your previous entries to see just how far you've come on your personal gratitude journey.

Allow yourself some time now to flip back to the start of this journal and remind yourself of why you decided to pick it up in the first place. Whatever the reason may have been, have you noticed anything different about yourself or your worldview between that moment and now? Do you feel happier, or have a more positive outlook than you used to? Or have you not really noticed much of a change in your overall mood? Have you left a few entries throughout the book blank as you've been unsure what to write there? Fear not, the good thing about this journal is that there is no deadline or time frame to work toward, nor is there any pressure to complete every single entry. This journal is here for you to pick up as and when you choose, so you can always go back to those blank entries should the mood strike. Gratitude should not be a chore, it should naturally become part of your life from here on out – we've just given you a few pointers to get you heading in the right direction.

> *"Gratitude turns what we have into enough, and more. It turns denial into acceptance, chaos into order, confusion into clarity... It makes sense of our past, brings peace for today, and creates a vision for tomorrow"*
>
> **MELODY BEATTIE**

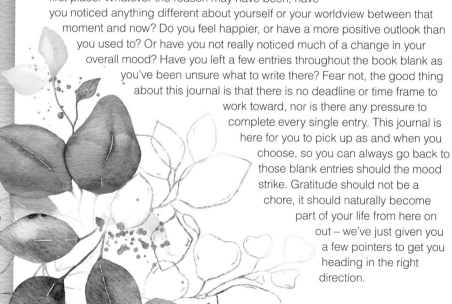

The first day of the rest of your life

You may have reached the end of the journal and run out of pages to fill in, but that doesn't mean your gratitude journey ends here – this is just the beginning. You are now equipped with all of the tools that you need to know about gratitude in order to apply it to every aspect of your life. Maybe you've learned something new about your career that you didn't realize you were thankful for? Or have you made peace with an element of your past? Perhaps you've got a newfound appreciation for your commute? Whatever it may be that you are now grateful for, try to remind yourself of these things when the going gets tough. The journal is now (hopefully) full to the brim with the many positives in your life, so when you find yourself in a moment of despair or sadness, use what you have learned to your advantage – you are now equipped with a handy tool. Flip back through the pages that you have filled in and remind yourself of everything that enriches your life, brings a smile to your face and fills your heart with joy.

There is no limit to gratitude

Over the course of writing in this journal, you will have discovered that gratitude is boundless. We can apply it to all aspects of our lives to help drive us to an overall feeling of happiness. By continuing to apply the basic principles of gratitude to your day-to-day life, you can focus your attention on how truly wonderful life can be.

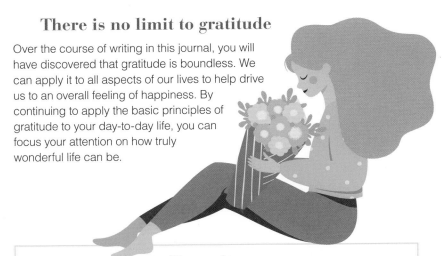

Pass it on

Maybe you've reached the end of this journal and feel such an overwhelming shift in your overall happiness that you wish to share what you've learned with others. So much of our lives involves sharing: we share memories, moments and belongings with one another, but you can also share skills and life lessons too. Do you have someone in mind who you believe is struggling? Could they also benefit from experiencing more gratitude in their life? One of the greatest pleasures in life comes from helping others, so why not share the key lessons you have learned with them? Your advice could help them to take the first steps of their very own gratitude journey.

In a world with so much uncertainty, choose joy

As Confucius once taught: "The green reed which bends in the wind is stronger than the mighty oak which breaks in a storm." Life can throw us some curveballs from time to time, but gratitude teaches us that we, too, can bend where we once might have felt we would break. Use your newfound gratitude as an invaluable tool to help deal with life's pressures and propel yourself forward in a more positive direction. There is so much to be grateful for in life – you just have to continue the practice of setting aside the time to notice it all.

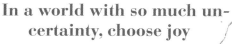

It's all because of you

Finally, take a moment to thank yourself for undertaking this gratitude journey in the first place. Be proud of making time to better yourself, for casting aside the negativity and choosing to focus on the positives in life. We often forget to look inward and appreciate the things we do and achieve on a daily basis. You are the master of your own destiny in many ways, and it's important to recognize that – acknowledge it and be grateful for yourself.

 # Reflections

How has keeping a gratitude journal changed you?
Reflect on how differently you feel now compared to when you began the journal

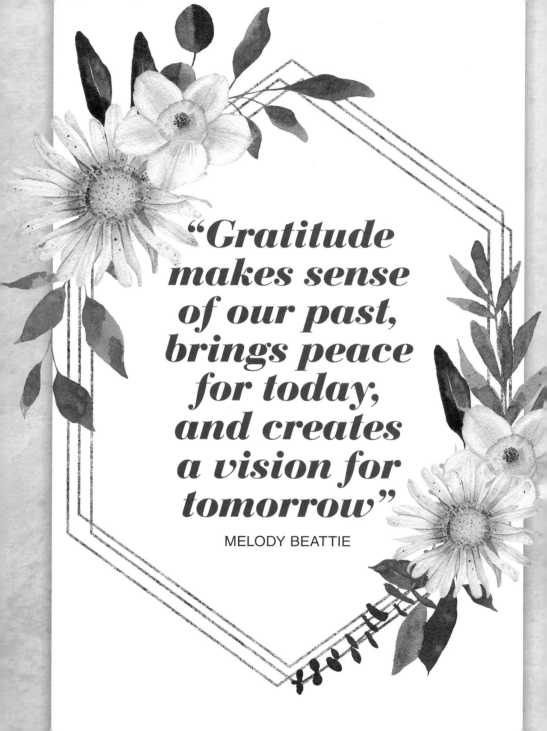

"Gratitude makes sense of our past, brings peace for today, and creates a vision for tomorrow"

MELODY BEATTIE

Reflections
on
Gratitude
Journal

ISBN 978-1-64178-171-8

Fox Chapel Publishing makes every effort to use environmentally friendly paper for printing.

© 2023 by Future Publishing and Quiet Fox Designs, *www.QuietFoxDesigns.com*, an imprint of Fox Chapel Publishing Company, Inc., 903 Square Street, Mount Joy, PA 17552.

Original content reproduced or translated from *Gratitude Journal*, a publication by Future Publishing Limited, a Future plc group company, UK 2022. Future Publishing Limited owns or licenses the mark.

FUTURE

Used under licence. All rights reserved.

For more information about the Future plc group, go to *http://www.futureplc.com*.

Future PLC Team
Editor: Sarah Bankes
Designer: Emma Wood
Compiled by: Jessica Leggett & Lora Barnes
Senior Art Editor: Andy Downes
Head of Art & Design: Greg Whitaker
Editorial Director: Jon White
Contributors: Julie Bassett, Natalie Denton, Laurie Newman, Dan Peel, Jackie Snowden
Cover images: Thinkstock

Fox Chapel Publishing Team
Managing Editor: Gretchen Bacon
Design and Production Manager: David Fisk
Copyeditor: Christa Oestreich

We are always looking for talented authors and artists. To submit an idea, please send a brief inquiry to acquisitions@foxchapelpublishing.com.

Printed in China
First printing